Best Wishes
Mary
from the [illegible]
Dara

"In *A Map of This World*, Dara McLaughlin's expertly worded, well-juxtaposed poetic images belie her courage in a war that few of us even notice. With her nimble mind, she caresses the reader's emotions, lulling him to peace but not to sleep, to understanding without remorse. She wishes not to establish within us a sense of irrevocable guilt, but to beam those of us who are "Temporarily Able-Bodied" from our current world of cynicism and unthinking cruelty into one where all people are accepted as equals.

We get a new view of "Public Places," the importance and agony of replayed memories in "Reebok Shrine," a wheelchair view of "Butts, Bellies, Belts, and Handbags," and a necessary earful of "Twenty-Two Stupid Things to Say to a Crip." These are the lessons most of us have needed forever. May we learn them half as well as Dara has written them."

Harvey Stanbrough
Editor, The Raintown Review
Nominee for the 1999 Pulitzer Prize for Letters

"We need to learn to live alongside persons with a disability, people of color, women, with anyone. . . . To realize that the 'other' is not they, but us, all of us, is a big step in the right direction."

Karen Stone
Awakening To Disability

"It is not that we, as persons with disabilities, want to be like the able-bodied any more. Simply, we cannot revert to our former selves or change our bodies. We want, instead, to create a new consciousness and thinking for society...and invite the able-bodied to share it with us."

André Dubus
Meditations from a Moveable Chair

"If you prick us, do we not bleed?"

William Shakespeare
The Merchent of Venice

A Map of This World

A Map of This World

Dara McLaughlin

River's Edge Press

I wish to thank Bette Casteel, Barbara Furr, Judy Fitzpatrick, Lee Perew, and Hope Bussey-MacKenzie of the writing group, STIMULUS, for their extraordinary editing and continuous support; Jeff Bryan, for his guidance in graphic design, his professional advice, and for showing me "the ropes;" Harish Sharma, for his unending encouragement and confidence in my work; Mike Bonner for his expert computer skills; my mother, Elaine Cacciato, for her patient listening ear through each step of this book; Alex Jacobs for showing me how to strengthen cultural identity through the arts, and my disabled friends and cohorts for sharing experiences and being an enthusiastic, authentic cheering section.

The author gratefully acknowledges the editors of the following publications in which some of these poems have appeared:
"Ode to Legs" *The Raintown Review* and *Pogos Polio News;*
excerpt of "Ode to Legs" *Poet's Market 1999* for *The Raintown Review;*
"Yes, The Paralyzed Girl Can Have Babies" *Very Large Array Anthology*;
"Temporarily Able-Bodied," "Staring Back," "The Exact Color of My Pubic Hair" *the rag;* "Heaven and Hell" *The Enabled Writer;*
"Heaven and Hell" *The Voice;* and The City of Albuquerque and The Albuquerque Museum for their program *"Disability Culture Night"* where most of these poems were read to an audience and televised with a premier reading of "Ode to Legs."

Front cover photograph: Michael Tabor
Back cover photograph: Kim Jew

Composed in *Minion* by J.B. Bryan.
Printed by Thomson-Shore
on acid-free recycled paper using soy inks

ISBN 0-9672342-0-4
Library of Congress Number 99-93424

River's Edge Press
2572 Sandia Loop NE
Rio Rancho, New Mexico 87124

For
Santo, Marla, and Daina
raised by a wheelchair mom
and we did fine

This collection is dedicated to the death of prejudice,
segregation, oppression, and discrimination.

This is the way and how I live.
Let me draw you a map of this world in true words. . .

CONTENTS

ADDENDUMS

Many years ago I said,
"If I ever lose my ability to walk
I'll kill myself
yes, I would have to—
don't try to stop me."

Then I became paralyzed
lost the use of my legs
and because I became paralyzed
it became necessary
to change the proclamation to:
"If I stay paralyzed
and lose the ability to use my hands and arms
if I become a quad
I'll kill myself
it's just the way it has to be—
don't try to stop me."

After several bouts of chemotherapy
I lost the use of my hands and arms
re-evaluation time:
"If I stay paralyzed
and can't use my hands and arms
and I also become blind
I'll kill myself—
don't
        try to stop me . . . ."

COBALT BLUES

Lying perfectly still, hospital gown doesn't warm me
the table colder still and hard
to lie on in any comfort
the tech leaves the room
the doctor leaves the room
the door marked with the triple-blade fan
shuts tight enough not to let the rays slip out
can't let the rays slip out
and hurt someone.

They look in through a window
four serious eyes, fingers pushing buttons
the robotics of machines
begin the work on my body.

Every day is like this
I, the guppy in a glass
they, cancer killers wielding
the great weapon Cobalt 60
I, the patient patient not wanting to die
they, sharp shooters of the invisible
wondrous possible cure precision-aimed
at the target—my chest
then arcing to cut an invisible circle
the perfect slice.

Lying perfectly still, still cold
still willing the miracle of cancer begone
it's almost Thanksgiving
they talk about turkeys
I joke they could "cook 'em right here"

I touch the burned-crisp skin
on my collarbone, breastbone
and believe it would actually work.

I slide off the table, slightly dizzy
a little nauseous
walk away till tomorrow
not knowing these rays take more than just cancer
not knowing these rays lead indiscriminate lives
not knowing that when a few months pass
there will be the moment when
I slump straight to the floor in a flawless heap
never to walk again.

I slide off the table and walk from that room
till tomorrow and tomorrow
when I will go back to lie still
for more damage.

ODE TO LEGS

I

Was it nature's reckless throw of indiscriminate die
part of a grand, irreversible plan
or did I share a night or two
hunkered down with the devil?

The roughest days are days of anguish when the consequences
of this wheelchair assault me . . . violent turbulent tempests
thrashing me whipping me ripping at my
loosened seams, waiting for spill
The calm days are lonely, endless
longing to walk again
the balm of sleep the antidote
if only for the night.

In dreams I dance to calypso
I dance with the wind I dance with clouds
unbridled dizzy with motion
manic dervish in a spell of rapture
undulating bones clicking blood pumping
a woman crazed with crazy joy
If a wheelchair appears in the
corner of my nocturnal stage
I don't (won't!) let it cripple my ethereal life
with one quick slash—I chop the corner off
It falls into oblivion, screaming
I crave my opiate dream-world like an addict.

Every day my worth is called to question
by a piteous world where even the perfect are
pummeled with messages that they are not perfect enough

a world so swollen with physical adoration
one could easily come to believe
that it is the body, not the soul, which is holy. A condemnation
magnified on bodies broken, twisted, different.

The rooms under my roof accommodate me well
not a single step to climb
epitome of accessibility sparing me
from the profusion of protrusions
barring me from the other world
the world which lurks outside my door
waiting to take me on.

In this sanctuary, my asylum
I retreat to romance in my head
intoxicate myself with fantasies of stepping out
body unlocked and free, stretching from earth to sky in one thin line
in the driveway: the poke of gravel under my feet
on the beach: the grit of sand between my toes
on the street: the tap of my own shoes striking ground
fantasies of bending, crouching, picking the weed and the tulip
feeling muscles stretch, respond
feeling muscles feeling. Standing up again.

I also call to order my adversities; I line them up
and shoot them one by one—shoot them—bang! —you're dead.

There is no glory in paralysis.

II

At the onset of my body's slow disintegration
    I used a cane, struggled to stay balanced
    half my body dipped in dry ice
    closing in on itself, smothered in pain
    my mind spinning wildly on the precipice of suicide
    my head in the lion's mouth   tempting   teasing
    one foot over the edge.   Catch me if you can. . . .

Then one day as I sat at my table of half-eaten breakfast, I rose leaning on my cane
suddenly, I had the legs of a fish—
    the walls, the windows, the sink, and stove
    shot up toward the ceiling in a streak as I plunged to the floor
    the blue tablecloth followed like a shroud
    landing with a crash of cold coffee, toast crusts and me.

then the room went still and I went still and only a saucer rolled around dizzily only a saucer moved then came to a quick stop in a corner swatted by an invisible hand my hands spread wide pressing the tile's pattern into the floor my chest a weakening cage around a heart about to burst the house as silent as heavy snow

And somewhere outside, a dog howled.

III

My poetry and journals
exploded with passion, fleshing out
the devastation of what was to be
a life-long unrelenting albatross, dagger beak and rapier claws
hooked savagely into my bleeding spine
In thick, black calligraphic letters
a gold-edged journal page: "In life I cannot walk,
in death I will rise and fly." Tears stream crimson with blood
pour deep enough to drown in
survival of the fittest. If this is so—let me go
this business of loss leaves me wasted.

When your legs fall into a deep sleep
unmoving, near dead
you are the embodiment of a blatant
physical flaw, a visible derangement
you are an ambassador of human tragedy
symbol of vulnerability, uncertainty
of what the future holds tomorrow or twenty years from now.
Some people stare.
Others look away.

I have wrestled with despair and torn at my own limbs
fingernails on fire, hammering fists
bestial lamentations piercing the night
a savage enraged
I've watched the fangs of disease devour my flesh piecemeal
I've damned the gods I've implored their mercy
prone, pathetic at their feet, bargaining
wailing in the face of powerlessness
a beggar.
I've spent hours, days, weeks,
insane with desperation
madly kissing my folded knees
that they might glean life from my lips.

IV

How have I survived? I'm sure of only this
    there are times of peace of heart, of feeling free—
Floating on the water's surface
    light as an empty paper cup
    holding onto nothing
    needing nothing but my breath.
Driving my car
    smooth forward motion
    the wind in my hair, the sun in my eyes.
Lying close and soft
    in my lover's arms.
These are the hours of resuscitation
    life breathed back into me.

A white flag billows from my upraised fist
    waving surrender to the grief of losing
    my legs.   My legs.
    The grief of losing my legs.

At last, my days and nights are filled with new perspectives
    reinvention   I'm busy
    honing resilience, molding a new life
                                    hands wet with the clay of liberation.

hope

endless   endless

hope.

V

At one time, I thought this poem should end
with "endless hope'"
as if hope is the best there can be
as if hope is good enough. Untrue.
Hope alone is cowardice
resignation with an optimistic twist
without contribution, prayer, focus of the tender kind
hope is hopeless.

When life betrays you
sinks it's thin, sharp teeth into your flesh and won't let go
you flail or fight or feel defeated
then summon the gods
Call clear out to heaven in the voice you'd reserved for heaven
before you were born
Call out in the blackest part of night, no star in sight
no moon, no hope, no friend, no lucky charm in your pocket
Call out in that voice you don't recognize
to the place of mercy you're unable to see
with a will to survive that emerges from the essence of your soul
Shear the blue-black night with your song
send ribbons of platinum song shimmering
into that dark night

And you will survive.
And you will make a life.
And you will know one fundamental truth—
You are whole.

PUBLIC PLACES

novenas

Black-sleeved elderly ladies appear from nowhere
Pobrecita! Que lastima!
they promise me novenas
kiss my forehead, kiss my cheek, mumble
words sounding sorrowful, words of woe
pleading words, words of mercy
Lo siento!
Lo siento mucho!

the kids

"Look out! Look out! Justin, Kate, Curt,
Sally, Tony, Maria, Miguel, Miguel! . . . "
parents yank their kids out of
my way (although they were never in it) in the grocery store
the theater, parking lot, pizza place, park, plaza
as if I'm harnessed to a tractor gone berserk
as if I am Danger—run like hell!
as if I require the parting of the great Red Sea.

The children? The children become wild-eyed, confused
stiff, as questions well in their fresh eyes
and I am not allowed to sate them
and I am not allowed to come too close
here the distortion begins
this is the fear instilled, the child changed
the myth perpetuated, the sharp seed of prejudice
sowed.

the jeans

I pay for my jeans at the K-Mart check-out
pull two bills out of my wallet
a twenty and a ten
hand them over to Melodee, a gum-chewing cashier
the register coughs and opens
Melodee smacks me right across the forehead
forking out the change to my companion
"The money's mine, Mel-o-dee!"
I pluck the cash mid-air
a talent I derived by watching hawks claim sparrows
Melodee draws in her chin, snaps a pink 'no problem' bubble
no giggle of embarrassment, or flush of cheek, or "sorry"
she bags the jeans, but hands them
to me.

the john

The stall door won't close behind me (again)
in the bathroom at the airport
not enough room in the handicapped stall (again)
to fit a whole wheelchair
the door pushes in and stays in and I am mostly out
I observe averted eyes, conduct my usual procedure
transfer to the toilet, exposed, pants around the ankles
slide a plastic stick between my legs
the throw-away catheter I paid a dollar for
in other words—a buck a pee
a woman watches from the mirror over the sink
(what does she think she sees?)
I review my choices—I can ignore her
or say, "want to take notes?"
I can—hell—I can say a lot of things

I have a whole damn repertoire to choose from
but don't.   She looks like an "Innocent"
she looks like me years ago.

leaving the house

I tell myself stay buoyant
remember humor the great diffuser
I conjure up the confidence that loves
to hide in folds and crevices of memory
I expect the unexpected also the expected.

Then I leave the house.

Never tell a disabled person you thought you had problems
till you met them.

THE EXACT COLOR OF MY PUBIC HAIR

It isn't right that a stranger—
no—several strangers at a time
anyone who happens to be in the public bathroom
same time as me
with that stall door wide open
with that half-assed attempt at access
with that disregard for dignity
it isn't right that they should know, no—
it isn't right that they should know
the exact color of my pubic hair.

GRAND PRIZE WINNER

"And the grand prize winner is—this is the moment we've all been waiting for—the grand prize winner is . . . Dara McLaughlin! Where are you Dara McLaughlin?

There she is!

Ms. McLaughlin . . . come on up! Come right up here on stage so we can all see you as we tell you all about the grand prize you have just won. That's right, up those steps and over here by me. You must be excited, Ms. McLaughlin, so here we go. Are you ready? The grand prize is . . . let's open the curtain . . . A Wheelchair!

What the hell is going on? I didn't want to be here.
I didn't ask to be here.

Yes, Ms. McLaughlin this wheelchair is Quickie's lightweight titanium sports model, with a custom backrest, fast-lock brakes, contour cushion and many more distinguishing features. And you have twelve exciting colors to choose from. But that's not all, Ms. McLaughlin, that's not all . . .

This must be a joke. If this is a joke, it isn't funny. I have children.
They're waiting for me. They depend on me.

You will also receive a lifetime guarantee of physical therapy with the therapist of your choice and a thirty-year supply of size fourteen-french catheters from Continental Laboratories, the world's finest catheters. That's thirty years, you heard it right . . . fifty-four thousand, seven hundred and fifty catheters! But wait—it doesn't end there—we wouldn't send you off without the rest of your prize, Ms. McLaughlin. That's right, there's more. You have also won . . . wait till you hear this folks . . .

A Brand-New vocabulary!

I'll wake up and this will be over.
I'll wake up and this will be over.
I'll wake up and this will be over.

Yes, you'll be learning plenty of new words such as clonus, decubiti, sitting-tolerance, Lioresal, pressure equalization, bladder distention, transfer board, adaptive controls, urinary drainage systems, ADA regulations, and many more.

Get me out of here! I need to escape! There's been a mistake! There's been a mistake!

Is something wrong, Ms. McLaughlin? Well, you must be overwhelmed with excitement. Of course, you are. Who wouldn't be? Please, everyone, let's give our winner, Ms. McLaughlin, a nice round of applause. That's right. Let's hear it for Ms. McLaughlin!

She's speechless, folks . . . and who could blame her? All this excitement! Here, Ms. McLaughlin . . . Sit down!"

TWENTY-TWO STUPID THINGS TO SAY TO A CRIP

ignorance innocent and intentional
offences innocent and intentional

"Vitamins! Vitamins! That's what you need! The doctors told my grandmother she would never walk again so she started taking lots and lots of vitamins from this particular company and now she walks two miles a day even in winter and square dances every Friday night!"

"My sister's back was so bad that she couldn't get out of bed for a year and then someone told her about a yoga class that was being given at the book store for free so she took the class and drank herbal teas and y'know now she's teaching yoga and her back is better than it has been in her whole life and she even works at the book store so now she guides others whose bodies are out of rhythm with natural states of being and y'know I know she would love it if you called her to talk about your problem so she could help you. You never know, y'know?"

"What you need to remember is that this is your gift. Jesus Christ is your savior and he loves you enough to give you this gift so that you can help others. Afflictions are our gifts and we must be thankful for them. We have a prayer group that you should come to on Wednesday nights. We'll thank the Lord for his gift to you and the souls you are about to touch. Thank you, father."

mother in a store to her rambunctious child as she points to me:
"If you don't start behaving yourself, you'll end up like that."

"Can you, you know, *do* it?"

"All this is the result of something you did in one of your past lives and you're living the consequences in order to become a higher being. It's a karma thing. Maybe you were in a duel and shot the other guy and paralyzed him or . . . maybe you could've been a world-famous dancer but you were an alcoholic and wasted your potential by drinking yourself to death. Could be anything. I know this woman who does past-life regression. You should go see her. Aren't you dying to know what you did to cause this?"

"My uncle uses a wheelchair and we drag him all over the place."

"I know just how you feel, honey. I broke my leg in two places a couple years ago. Had to use a wheelchair for six months . . . imagine! I couldn't go nowheres. I couldn't do nothing but sit there for the whole six months. So I know . . . I know how hard it is to bear the cross—God bless you. I know first-hand."

"Wouldn't it be easier to walk?"

"Hey—watch out—you're gonna get a speeding ticket!"

"There's this monk in the Himalayan Mountains who does nothing but teach individuals who seek him out about their higher selves until they are no longer attached to their physical being and therefore the conditions of the body become insignificant. This should be of interest to you."

"You should get a horn on that thing!"

"Don't drink and drive! Get it? Drink—drive?!"

"I know this one doctor who works absolute miracles. He worked on that one singer, you know, the one who broke his spine or something and came back one hundred percent. I forget his name. So this doctor is the one who got him back on stage. I don't know how exactly but I'll try to get his name for you."

"You're lucky you get to sit down . . . my feet are killing me."

"We were making significant progress with research in the area of spinal cord injury and related maladies such as Parkinson's and Alzheimer's Disease until Reagan and Bush terminated all fetal cell transplant experiments. Now the Danes are way ahead. Maybe the Germans, too. I'd be pissed if I were you."

"If I was you and they told me I couldn't play no more football . . . I'd off it, man."

"Tell the truth, no shit, you're one easy rape."

"Mommy, why is that lady in a wheelchair?" "She's tired, honey."

"I feel so sorry for you. I know how hard it is to get around in a wheelchair. When I take the baby out in the stroller and have to look for those ramp-things, I think . . . what a pain."

"We had to do this one experiment in school where we had to pick a handicap and pretend to have it for two days. I picked getting confined to a wheelchair and went to the mall and the library and ate at Raimondo's. I guess we do need more access. But all in all it was kind'a fun."

"What do you think this condition brings you that you can't get in any other way? Why do you think your subconscious mind chose paraplegia to express what you need from life? How does needing to be in a wheelchair help you? Does it help you avoid adult responsibilities? Does it fulfill your need for attention?"

"You're lucky you're alive. Some people are dead."

BEING HERE

notes for a nondisabled person who pretends to know

I sit with a cold bottle of dark beer and a book of dark poetry. The view from here—The Rio Grande, The Bosque, The Sandias straight ahead. See the long-awaited storm thunder in from the north? Great oceanic clouds, wolf-gray, filling the sky with shameless portent. Feel the wind pick up, increase, increase, till the desert floor lifts in a flurry obliterating view. Tumbleweed big as hay bales bounce with good speed piling up like too many children. Huge raindrops plop onto the sandy earth; the wind so savage it borders unbearable.

Watch the rain continue to fall. Feel the wind continue to blow. See my skirt and hair whipped and beaten? Breaths drawn in desperate gulps? Listen to the music of the wind creating long, mournful whistles as it passes the mouth of the beer bottle. Listen to its wide howling notes as it wails around the corner of the house like a ghoul. If I take the brakes off this chair and let go, wind will push me forward or backward until I recover control.

Rain soaks into my skin and when my skin is wetted enough, rain rolls in clever veins of water, ever-changing designs of water, thin shiny snakes of water on top of my skin. I don't care that I'm drenched and chilled. I hold my head up, face the wind head-on, open my mouth inhaling the storm deeply, fully.

You understand, don't you? About excitement. Involvement. Adventure. The thrill of melding your own blood and ivory bones with the hot-blue electric tension of storms. Listening from the inside. Absorbing whipped-up clean smells, dirt smells, earth smells, face to face with the power of something invisible; a devil or an angel wreaking havoc, wielding the power of danger in the shape of a storm.

But I need to go indoors for a minute. I open the door, go inside, fight a wicked fight with the wind to get the door closed. Fight and push with all my strength. All my will. At last. It shuts.

Instant transition. The house is quiet, eerily still. It protects me; I'm safe, untouched. Back in the belly. Heartbeat. Breathing is effortless. Water runs in rivulets from my hair, down my bare cold arms and puddles to the floor. My hair and skirt now unmoving. Did you feel that switch? Did you notice how quick it was? Like a bee sting? Like a lightning bolt? Like the snap of a neck? Now look—look out of the window—

You *see* the storm.
You *see* what the wind tosses.
You *see* the effects of rain on sand.

> You *read* about storms in books.
> You *watch* storms in movies.
> You *hear* stories of storms.
> You *imagine* being in storms.
> But you cannot *be* in a storm unless you *are* in a storm.
> You cannot ***be*** here unless you ***are*** here.

Don't tell me you know what it's like.

LIST

physically challenged   less-abled   disabled   poster boy   crip
handicapped   poster girl   geek   vegetable   differently-abled
super-crip   otherly-abled   roller   welfare-drain   welfare-leech
welfare-choker   geekdejure   wheeler   wheelie   invalid
Jerry's kids   patient   wheelchair-bound   victim   in a wheelchair
misfit   crippled   pity-date   disfigured   spazz   gimp   gimpy
physically impaired   pretzel   nonwalker   special   chair
ironsides   sidewinder   quad   para   limited   inspiration
physically limited   you people   those people   physically restricted
quasimodo   impaired   half-man   half-woman   half-person
freak   mendicant   unfortunate   sorry state   sickly   stick people
disposable   brave   courageous   tragedy   pitiable   marred
confined to a wheelchair   condemned to a wheelchair
stuck in a wheelchair   cursed   damaged   enfeebled
convalescent   paralytic   lame   freak   freak show   freak of nature
poor thing   impeded   burden   burden on society   disadvantaged
debilitated   immobile   palsied   paraplegic   quadriplegic   maimed
oddity   non-ambulatory   incurable   imprisoned   incomplete
broken   not whole   touched by the devil   sick   charity case
defective   deficient   fate worse than death   incapacitated
tax burden   survivor   all-boogered-out   dysfunctional
too much trouble   better off dead   not dead yet   spinner
makes your heart bleed   icon of tragedy   pathetic   handi-capable
mobility impaired   people with differing abilities   pitiful

and the list goes on

HAIKU

Patch of ice
the wheelchair can't do it
I stay in the car

Seven steps
same as a brick wall
same as a deep ravine

For just one instant
the eyes convey his pity
irrevocable

Deep woods
leg-trap snaps bone
the crack—the scream—the scream

Contemplating
the illusion
of stillness

Searching in cold air
the wind finds its own music
in dead tree hollows

my face

in the rain

hiding tears

my face

in the rain

hiding tears

my face

the rain

tears

my face

rain

tears

face

rain

tears

face

tears

NECESSARY ACTIONS

Finally got home from five months in rehab
where I learned to live from the "chair"
where I first confronted the grief
of losing the use of my legs

I waited for the husband to leave with the kids for the day
that wasn't hard, now that I lived in a body different
he could hardly wait to be away from me
couldn't bear to see me using the wheelchair
couldn't bear it out of too much love or too much repulsion
the divorce was a nasty one

it happened on a Sunday
alone, at last alone, I wheeled into our closet
a closet full of shoes
wriggling from chair to floor
sat for a long time, sat among my shoes
then anger whipped up, pain grabbed me by the throat
and every shoe with a heel I hurled across the bedroom
hitting walls, smashing the mirror, breaking a lamp
shoes, shoes with heels, useless, freaking goddamned shoes

later, on a better day, I bagged my shoes and gave them
away, a pair to this one, a pair to that one
Cookie loved my red shoes, the one from the forties
strappy and high, deep red like garnet
I gave her my shoes, a telling moment
not your ordinary lend and borrow, not your
ordinary give-away
I wondered how I would feel the first time I see
her walk in my shoes, those shoes, her shoes

FIRESIDE

Always when I sit
beside the comfort of a home-fire
logs ablaze, spitting heat
sparks unpredictable as life
it is then I achieve clarity of thought
blatant honesty, a time of reckoning
a time of listening to my own soul.

I think what my life would have been
not needing a wheelchair
would it be like BC—Before Chair?
would I have lost out on the rich unique
slant, the perspective I paid dearly for?

What would it be like
to wake tomorrow, stand up and walk
how would I handle it?
how would my life change?
I contemplate desiring it
and choose not to.

If "the cure" arrived would I take it?
   maybe
what would it cost in time, pain, risk
how much life would I have to give
to walk—what is the trade-off ratio
how much cure is really cure?
if I say "yes," it's what I want
not what I need.

I think about never walking again
of using a chair, being paralyzed
for all the rest of the days of my life
here there are no questions
no what ifs, no transitions
I will live as I live now
and it will be all right
no profound sadness, no disappointment
no regret
love itself and living fully are my essence
no one, no thing can paralyze that.

Light dances with shadows on the walls
I feel the heat and power
of my own fire.

A FAREWELL TO LEGS

Farewell to legs
  the way I used to use them

Given enough time
you realize the "chair" is a tool
not a crutch
not a thing to hate
not a thing to hide
given enough time, the "chair"
becomes second nature,
graceful, really, in its own way
an extension of yourself
like a thick coat you've worn for years
a settling in takes place
and the days of missing walking days
gain more space between

Farewell to legs
  the way I used to use them.
Farewell.

ALIVE 'N' KICKIN'

I kick my love in the middle of the night
a spasm or two, maybe three
part of the landscape
at least he knows I'm still alive.

He breathes rhythms into the curve
of my ear all night long
his baritone snore
is comfort, part of the landscape
at least I know he's still alive.

Even under Morpheus' spell, we communicate
even under Morpheus' spell, we know one another
to be alive and safe
he and I are alive
and safe
he and I are alive
and safe
alive and safe and kickin'.

HAPPY BIRTHDAY, BABY

She is five today; she wears her "zoo" dress
cheeks flush with excitement
hair sparkles from a fresh shampoo.

She is five and darling
she stands on a chair to reach the bakery cake
marble-sized plastic balloons rise from its center
pink candles shrink from flame.
She is five; she is my daughter, this is her day
and I love her beyond understanding.

And when the birthday song is sung
and it's time to make a wish and time to blow the candles out
daughter clasps hands to chin
inhales fully, spends her wish—
"I wish mommy could walk again."
the candle's flame disappears
in a soft spark while family and friends
quick-look to me—caught—
in that space between love and grief.

YES, THE PARALYZED GIRL CAN HAVE BABIES

Yes, the paralyzed girl can have babies—
    Even after the disease, event, tragedy, bad luck, karma, wrong place-wrong time, will of god, way it was meant to be, accident, twist of fate, harrowing experience, screw-up, fuck-up, way life works, consequence, tragedy, mishap, misfortune, serious blow, adversity, catastrophe, calamity, heart breaker, fluke of nature.

The answer is simple.

Yes, the paralyzed girl can have babies
    because she's a woman, because she has a womb
    because she's the same as the non-paralyzed girl
    having sex, making love, making out,
    and if you come right down to it
    it doesn't take much more than a lucky connection
    to reproduce so, yes—
even paralyzed girls have babies.

TEMPORARILY ABLE-BODIED (TAB)

Two guys in a bar. Both have wheelchairs.
First guy says to the second guy
"What are you?"
Other guy says, "C-5*. You?"
First guy says, "T-8**. Bullet."
Second guy lifts his beer, a little. "Motorcycle."
That's it. Nothing funny about these two guys in a bar.
They speak the same language, understand
without words the stories and history and all the bits and pieces
of one another's existence. Nothing funny.

Two guys in a bar. They have wheelchairs. Having a good ol' time.
Just that afternoon the first guy's girlfriend left him for a "Walker."
He knew it would happen some day. Today was the day.
He drowns the disengagement in another beer.
The second guy celebrates another month at the job.
It won't last long; he's too complicated, too much a symbol of tragedy.
Life's tough enough without reminders.

Two guys in a bar. Both have wheelchairs.
They look around, take in the scenery, the only two guys in the bar
who know the meaning of TAB. The only two guys in the bar who
know that every other guy in the bar is a TAB.
Nothing funny about that either.

*C-5 an injury at the 5th cervical vertebra

**T-8 an injury at the 8th thoracic vertebra

REEBOK SHRINE

—for Ange

Fifteen seconds left in the game
          fourteen . . . thirteen . . . twelve . . .
                    BAM!
He slams against the sideboard   Snaps his neck
Crumples to the ice   Lies completely still
That's it.   Done.

Now his sneakers stand propped on his dresser.
The Reeboks. The ones he wore to the game
on his last walk. The Reeboks right there
under jersey #44 hanging on the wall. Those were the days.

It'll take a few years before he comes around,
before he settles into his new life, takes pride in it.
And he might. He might.
For now he lies in bed with dreams
he lies in bed with memories
he lies in bed on constant replay—
          fourteen . . . thirteen . . . twelve
                    BAM!

POEM FOR A CAN OPENER

I want to open a can of tuna and share it with someone I love

I want to open my fist to find a nugget of fine poetry in my palm

I want to open a sandwich shop in Costa Rica
but probably won't because I don't want it enough

I want to open my mouth and have magnificent words
pour out like champagne and moonlight

I want to open a vein and clamp it shut at the last moment
just to see what it's like

I want to open a bottle of expensive wine on a pier at night
with that perfect partner who adores me and stays true

I want to open the sky and see for myself
what hovers over it

I want to open the eyes and ears and hearts and minds
of the kids in juvenile detention centers by teaching them poetry

I want to open my grandparents' kitchen back door
see them alive again, have them offer me oatmeal cookies with raisins
and stories

I want to open myself up to the probability that I
will remain single for the rest of my life

I want to open a newspaper and read
a declaration of world peace signed in blood
by every country on the planet

I want to open an oyster shell
and find the key to happiness

I want to open a checking account
and not be afraid the IRS will
extract from it at their will

I want to open an open discussion
about why strangers and mild acquaintances
think just because I use a "chair"
they can ask me if I can have an orgasm

I want to open my closet and see that someone
has cleaned it

I want to open my garage and see that someone
has cleaned it

I want to open my mind and see that someone
has cleaned it

I want to open the tomb of Nebuchadnezzar
poke his ancient bones and ask:
What were you thinking, Neb?

I want to open a daily column in the newspaper
that lists names, addresses, and phone numbers
of all able-bodied people who illegally
park in the handicapped spots

I want to open a book to the page that tells
the difference between want and desire

I want to open my heart to anyone who has ever hurt me
but I don't have all the steps down yet

I want to open a theater that has disabled persons
playing disabled persons, Indians playing Indians

I want to open the first public school that teaches
the truth about life and the truth about love

I want to open all the drawers in the department store
that hold all the cosmetics, and spend days
experimenting with the stuff

I want to open the fridge and just once, find
not one single solitary thing growing blue fuzz

I want to open my lungs to pure, unadulterated
air

I want to open the heads of Stephen Hawkins
and William Shakespeare
to see what makes them you-know

I want to open all my senses at the same time
to 100% capacity
without drugs

I want to open all the files kept secret
on the JFK assassination

I want to open all the files withheld
from adopted people wanting to know their heritage

I want to open the bridge between disability shame
and disability pride, have everyone cross over
from shame to pride, then burn it

I want to open a can of tuna and share it with someone I love.

D: Here. I want you to read this poem and tell me what you think.

K: I like it. It's cool. Pretty clever.

D: Thanks. I had fun writing it.

K: There's one thing I don't get, though.

D: What's that?

K: Through the whole thing you never told about wanting to walk again.

D: It never occurred to me.

K: Are you going to add it on?

D: No. I don't need to. It's no longer part of the picture.

K: I'll never understand that.

D: If I could walk again someday, then great. But I don't have to anymore. I'm healthy, have a full life, lots of love around me and in me. The old need to walk simply faded until it disappeared.

K: And that's the truth?

D: That's the truth.

HEAVEN AND HELL

A Clarification for Misguided Concepts

It was an accident
the ordinary, everyday, unexpected
unpredicted twist of fate.

Now s/he's a wheelchair rider
a side-winding, land-roving, heaven and hell on wheels

s/he may be angry, s/he may have pain
but s/he doesn't need anybody's sympathy

s/he may be independent, s/he may do as she pleases
but s/he is not a hero, s/he's just living

s/he may take longer to get ready
s/he may take longer getting there
but s/he gets there all the same

s/he may do this different and sometimes that
but s/he gets it done, s/he makes it happen

s/he may deal with the deal
accept and overcome
but s/he is not an inspiration

s/he may smile, s/he may put you at ease
but s/he will not accept the label "cheerful"

s/he may be a curiosity, s/he may remind you of a tragedy
s/he may have unusual priorities
but s/he is not a spectacle, s/he is not on parade

s/he may sometimes hold a distant stare
which you may think must be depression
don't be fooled, s/he's thinking, thinking just like you do

s/he thinks and feels and dreams and does and doesn't
and will and won't with all the faults and all the virtues
of any human being

s/he's unique but hardly "special"
s/he's just your average, run-of-the-mill wheelchair rider
a side-winding, land-roving, heaven and hell on wheels.

BUTTS, BELLIES, BELTS & HANDBAGS

From this, the seated position
my view is rearranged from walking days
I have assumed the unsolicited honor of close-ups
of bellies—flat bellies, loose bellies, work-out bellies, belted bellies,
bare bellies, aproned bellies, growing bellies, jelly-bellies,
full bellies, empty bellies, groaning bellies, old bellies, young bellies,
dark bellies, light bellies, tattooed bellies, girdled bellies,
bellies holding babies.

On the opposite side of bellies
I see butts
multitudes of butts
jiggling butts, upscale butts, high butts, low butts,
muscular butts, well-dressed butts, aging butts,
youthful butts, butts that need attention, butts that don't,
round butts, flat butts, hard-working butts, butts that sit too much,
dancing butts, dragging butts, funny butts, shrinking butts,
butts of magnitude.
Someday I'll write a scholarly book called "Diversity of Butts."

Then belts—I see belts straight ahead straight
as the crow flies I see
cowboy belts, buckled belts, stretch belts, leather belts,
wide belts, narrow belts, custom belts, weaved belts,
designer belts, cheap belts, belts studded with turquoise,
belts declaring "god is love," belts with monograms,
belts with pagers, belts with cell phones, belts with loads of keys,
furry belts, old belts, new belts, belts in between,
shiny belts, dyed belts, belts that work, belts that don't,
belts with bellies hanging over.
I bet every belt made by man is a belt I've seen.

While butts and belts and bellies
stay where they belong (attached to a person)
handbags can be dangerous
handbags swing and rock and toss
they fling and hurl and heave
they launch and whirl and whip
yes, women have no grip
on where their handbags are in space
with no thought whatsoever they whack me in the face
they thump across my shoulder and hit me in the head
if there's a loaded shopping bag that's almost always next
another thwack, another whack, another black and blue
I've learned to see it coming, I've learned to be aware
I've relearned "duck and cover"
and put it to good use.

But times have changed and so have I
I've left behind those gruesome days
those days of weaving, wheeling, through
the labyrinth of bellies, the crazy maze of butts,
the birds' eye view of people's belts, the handbags that assault
I continue shopping
I'll always be a shopper
I continue shopping
but now I shop on-line.

STARING BACK

The sear of the stare, the double-take
the cease of a smile, the sudden grin
the gimpy gesture behind my back
I know them all
nothing's new, no big surprise, no original wit
sticks and stones may break my bones
but stares no longer hurt me.

To those of you who stare
I invite you to listen close—
some day, if should you join these ranks
(which you will if you don't die first)
you will be astounded by who it is that pulls you up
who steadies you and stands by you
who guides you to be strong
helps you hold your head up high.

To those of you who stare
we'll be staring back because of what we know
we'll be staring back to remember you
we'll be staring back so you'll remember us
when you stare, stare closely
we will be your mentors
we were here before you
and you will need us.

SOME MORNINGS

Some mornings
damn them
some mornings I forget

I unfurl my pillow, turn around
and there it is
the "chair," sitting there, waiting

the necessary demon—
empty until I shake my head free of dreams
slip out of bed to nestle my body into its curve

some mornings I remember
as soon as dawn declares itself
then it's business as usual

it's the mornings of forgetting
that bother my soul, force a transition
of the mind, the day begun with a silent uncomfortable slap

some mornings I forget
damn them
some mornings I forget.

In *A Map of This World*, I have addressed only some of the issues surrounding disability. A myriad more exist as any person with a disability can attest to. The issues are social, political, historical, medical, financial, economic, architectural, physical, sexual, philosophical, emotional, and spiritual. And we live them every day.

There is a long history of oppression and discrimination of disabled people which inevitably led to The Disability Rights Movement and the formation of Disability Culture. The Disability Rights Movement began in 1962, the day Ed Roberts wheeled through the doors of The University of California at Berkeley becoming their first severely disabled student after an arduous fight to pursue his right to education. Later, Roberts became the first executive director of The Center for Independent Living, director of California's Dept. of Vocational Rehabilitation, and founder of the World Institute on Disability with co-founders Judith Heumann and Joan Leon. There are many heroes of this Movement: Justin Dart Jr., world leader in disability rights and principal architect of the Americans with Disabilities Act (ADA) 1990, Robert Kafka, national organizer for ADAPT, and innumerable other advocates who have made profound changes for disability rights through many mediums including visual, literary, and performing arts.

Disability Culture is the collective identity and source of community, pride, and empowerment among disabled people. Like many other cultures, the culture of disability redefines old, negative images and transforms them into what our group truly is. Disability is not a tragic medical problem with pitiable circumstances but rather a state of the body which is different from the majority. Disability Culture has heroes, history, ancestors, a language, a true identity. Cheryl Marie Wade, a performance artist, says, "Disability Culture takes a figure such as Helen Keller and changes her from the child muttering 'wah wah' in *The Miracle Worker* (1962) to a social activist, writer, world traveler, and political figure."

People with disabilities must be recognized as functional, valuable citizens with much to contribute to society. We can all benefit from breaking through stereotypical thinking and breaking down the barriers of misconception about disability. Even if beliefs and attitudes are changed one by one, we are headed in the right direction.

A good friend and sister crip ends her correspondences with these words: "Move about in radiant beauty."

I like that.

Some Suggested Reading:

Pelka, Fred. *The ABC-CLIO Companion to The Disability Rights Movement.*
Santa Barbara: ABC-CLIO. Inc., 1997.

Dubus, André. *Meditations From a Movable Chair.*
New York: Alfred A. Knopf, Inc., 1998.

Fries, Kenny, ed. *Staring Back, The Disability Experience from the Inside Out.*
New York: Plume, 1997.

Hockenberry, John. *Moving Violations.*
New York: Hyperion, 1995.

Stone, Karen G. *Awakening to Disability, Nothing About Us Without Us.*
San Francisco: Volcano Press Inc., 1997.

Shapiro, Joseph P. *No Pity: People with Disabilities Forging a New Civil Rights Movement.*
New York: Times Books, 1994.

Milam, Lorenzo Wilson. *Crip Zen, A Manual For Survival.*
San Diego: MHO & MHO Works, 1993.

Keith, Lois, ed. *"What Happened to You?"*
New York: The New Press, 1996.